Charm Offensive

Winner of The Sexton Poetry Prize,
a note from Judge Lloyd Schwartz,
Pulitzer-prize winner

What a pleasure it has been reading the submissions for Eyewear's annual Sexton Prize, this year. Among the twelve finalists, any one of the manuscripts could have made a plausible winner. These entries were all intelligent, ambitious, serious, formally intriguing, often witty, and often quite moving.

But two remarkable manuscripts distinctly stood out for me: Ross White's *Charm Offensive* and Sarah Bridgins' *Death and Exes*. And after reading and re-reading them many times, I couldn't choose one over the other. Each one deserves publication and each one deserves first prize.

Perhaps, as Ross White says in the title of his introductory poem, 'I Like Too Many Things'. But in both cases, while these books are very different from one another, what they had in common was a truly individual and convincing voice. Every word seemed personal and deeply felt, as if both of these poets urgently needed to tell me what they were thinking. Not a single poem in either of these collections ended where I expected it to – as if each writer was engaged in the process of discovering in the course of a poem what it was they each had to say, not just merely producing good poems that sounded like other good poems. And both of these poets have their own quirkily humorous and ironic view of the world, and of themselves.

I admired them for seeming to take their poems more seriously than they took themselves. Nothing in either of these books feels either effortful or over-simplified, or predictable.

Elizabeth Bishop once wrote that the poetry she liked best shared the qualities of 'accuracy, spontaneity, mystery'. I found those qualities in both of these collections, and I am very pleased to have both Ross White and Sarah Bridgins share first prize.

My congratulations.

Charm
Offensive

ROSS WHITE

THE **BLACK SPRING**
PRESS GROUP

First published in 2023
by The Black Spring Press Group
Eyewear Publishing imprint
Maida Vale, London W9,
United Kingdom

Typeset and cover design by Edwin Smet

978-1-913606-62-6

*Publisher's note: This book won the 2019 prize and was due out in 2020,
but was delayed by the pandemic until 2023. We thank the poet for their patience.*

*The editor has generally followed American spelling and punctuation
at the author's request.*

BLACKSPRINGPRESSGROUP.COM

Ross White is a poet, publisher, and teacher from Durham, NC. He is the author of *Charm Offensive*, winner of the 2019 Sexton Prize, and three chapbooks. He is the director of Bull City Press, an independent publisher of poetry, fiction, and nonfiction, and the host of *The Chapbook*. He teaches creative writing and grammar at the University of North Carolina at Chapel Hill.

TABLE OF CONTENTS

I LIKE TOO MANY THINGS

to ever be satisfied with one. The giant squid and mountain lion
mesmerize me equally, as do other pairs: blackberry and watermelon,
puppies and kittens, underbrush and lichen, Larry Bird and Magic Johnson,
beer and White Russians, turkey and mutton, domestic and foreign,
polyester and cotton, dirty laundry and fresh linen, Incas and Mayans,
black holes and ions, sensory deprivation and cosmic vision.
I am a sort of griffon: head of a wanderer, heart of a dragon,
allegiance to neither. So my attention, battered, is often cloven,
and I, smitten with a new idea or fascinating button, appear a cretin.
But I am unruined. I speak a pidgin, but listen to the origins
of the words: a smidgeon of Korean, a smidgeon of Briton,
laden with an unburdened appreciation of living. My written
communications have the same enlightened tone, if you're bitten
with the same or similar affliction and others often listen
in bewilderment, as though it is in Latin, to what you consider common
sense. Otherwise, I beg your pardon. I could draw it for you in crayon.
There is a heaven. In it, all things are in pairs, or triplets, or sevens.

JUNK DRAWER

Photographs of the waterskiing versions of us,
the ones who went to Machu Picchu & Chunchucmil,
the selfish & long-haired & parasailing us,

now stuck together, gloss on gloss.
Deck of cards & Philips-head screwdriver,
cords & wires for gadgets I no longer own.

I drink a lot of chai now & do insufferable crosswords
& when I'm digging for a reading light
or alligator clip I'll linger on stray photos,

linger on younger you with such lavender nostalgia,
younger me with such disdain –
How stupid he looks in paisley! Those horn-rims! –

& I'll pull apart the pictures of you in a tiara & satin
& you at doing the cha-cha at a Waffle House
& you fellating a Ronald McDonald statue

& you'll seem newer to me than milk,
newer than a sleek foal,
though of course I have been your old horse for years.

Outside, rain will beat down the grass
until it bends lower than when it's fresh-cut,
vines will wrap green fingers around trunk & limb,

as if to pull the high branches down.
The arms of gravity never do the job fast enough.
Down birch, down oak. Down shed.

Down clapboard & down Tudor revival & down ranch.
That pull. We're getting older & we feel it,
even when so long ago doesn't feel so long ago.

We'll end up in soil & wormbelly & root system
& eventually we'll be in the fossil record
for scientists of a much older earth —

which will, to them, seem new & renewing —
to rummage around in, regarding our strata
for its clutter, its tires & smokestacks & bones.

MICHELANGELO'S *DAVID*

unlike the other Davids, has not yet defeated Goliath,
his sling limp over his shoulder.
Though scholars write papers on the tension
in his neck, the taut muscles,
he always seemed to me unthreatened,
his leg casually lifted, his right arm slack,
his gaze off in the distance.

I'm so often admonished to tell the truth
slant that I should know better
than to accept the first viewpoint
yet I've only just discovered that
the statue, chest out, begs to be looked at
from the angle he was placed in
by the Accademia's curators,
his abdomen lithe, his staggering perfection
suggesting that he sends the warning look
away, to a distant foe or city.

When I step to David's side,
into his line of sight, the crook in his arm
raises a muscle toward the enemy,
the hand swung low
clutches a weapon almost out of sight,
and war is in his white eyes.

Because we think we see the truth
but see it slant, we are quick to assume
we are not the aggressors, we mean no harm,
we do not wear the Philistines' armor,
we will never be felled simply by stones,
that God has not yet chosen
the instruments of our inevitable humiliation.

TWO SWANS

after Brigit Pegeen Kelly

I am keeping very still,
my pants hiked, my socks rolled down
over the mouth of my sneakers,
so limb leads can read my heart at an angle.
Shirtless, pressed flat to paper pulled
over the creaky plastic exam table.
The leads on my chest pump electrical information
to the EKG machine for interpretation.
The nurse says, *You seem a little anxious*
and I am. But how can she tell?
I am keeping very still.
The physician's assistant says,
Try thinking of something you enjoy
but I can't seem to think of anything.
A picture on the wall displays a proud,
healthy cartoon heart, bloodless
and stripped of its ventricles.
I am thinking of swans.
I don't enjoy swans, but here they are,
two, in the mental picture I'm supposed
to calm myself with, gliding towards each other
on a flat lake, a lake whose surface doesn't crease
for ripples, so calm that it might as well be ice,
until they almost meet, and in the negative space
between them, their craned necks form the outline
of a heart, a healthy cartoon heart.
I am keeping very still.
I was told electrocardiograms require stillness
for an accurate reading.
Sudden movement would upset
the machine. Sudden movement would scare away
the swans. Aside from breathing,

I haven't moved an inch.
I am reminding myself that I have to breathe,
that breathing does not preclude stillness,
that I was told to keep very still.
I am keeping very still.
The machine makes a *scree* sound,
printing a reading, then another.
I tell myself not to be humiliated
but I'm always humiliated with my shirt off,
this white belly.
I have resorted to jokes with my wife –
there's a baby kangaroo in this pouch I got,
or *Blackbeard hid his treasure here*
but you can't dig it out until I'm dead.
What are those leads digging out of me
and sending back for analysis?
I am keeping very still,
hoping keeping still won't be
a permanent condition.
There is someone outside the exam room.
I can hear the scrape of chart against door.
I know the light streaming in
the crack under the door is now broken
by two feet. I have looked at light
under enough exam room doors
to recognize that break, someone standing,
chart in hand, thinking about coming in,
thinking, *Again, this poor bastard.*
I would crane my neck
to see his feet's twin shadows but
I am keeping very still.
I am thinking of swans.
I am thinking of a dead doe's legs,
upturned, the white of her bloating belly
appearing, at a distance, to be two swans.

No, not dead; just a doe, upturned and still.
That's it, the nurse says.
I can get up, can dress, can wait, can watch
the twin shadows come, pause, go.
That's it, a new doctor, the last set of shadows,
says. I'm fine, I can put on my coat
and go home, can skip admit on my way out.
The printouts from the EKG machine,
drawings in an unsteady hand,
are the downward strokes of a feather,
a clumsy attempt at a wing.
And all that peaceful white space:
two swans stuck in ice.
I can go now, I can get off the table.
But I can't. I don't.
I am keeping very still.

DEAD FINCH

The dead finch on the porch:
perhaps the cat brought it as a trophy,

and placed it like a gift between the flowerpots.
Perhaps it simply laid down there,

as living things do when they finally transition
to being dead things.

A live finch leaves his perch on the power line
and flits to the side of the dead finch

where he stands and flips his head quickly
from side to side,

inspecting in a hundred directions
every facet of the dead finch's motionlessness,

as if calculating angles
by which they might escape together.

The live finch bolts into flight,
dipping just below the straightest path

to the birch across the street.
The live finch returns, chirps,

jerks his neck to examine the dead finch
from new vantages,

then flies again the concave arc to the birch.
And this repeats a fifth time, a tenth,

until in the distance a leaf blower roars
to life, and the live finch startles

and takes wing to the power line,
then to the distant midmorning sky.

QUAE NOCENT SAEPE DOCENT

My bow-legs crossed, I sat before someone I thought the great teacher.
His whole body a fist, he said, "Pain is the great teacher."

As sun rejects moon, as water rejects fire, one must reject a notion first
if one is ever to embrace it. The flower of denial, perhaps, the great teacher?

I wandered the museums of terra cotta soldiers and the mansions
of silence. I asked the ronin where I might find the great teacher.

I sent my dream-self to the rounded hovels at the edge of imagination.
I asked all the creatures in the dreaming where I might find the great teacher.

I learned to see the world through the eye of a needle, to shape sticks,
to sing mourning songs. I thought myself the envy of the great teacher.

But stone grew around my feet and held me fast as I became stone.
Then I believed for some years that humility was the great teacher.

In autumn evening, the outline of a woman broke the purple horizon.
She looked at me with such pity and asked if I had found the great teacher.

My ruin forgotten, I thawed. I built us a canoe, I painted figurines of ronin as gifts.
Her delight was rose-petal. I abandoned my search for the great teacher.

One cannot know incompletion until completed. Newly in love,
what need had I for the counsel of the great teacher?

It never occurred to me that I might undress my beloved and discover
the white blooms of scar across her back, shadows of the great teacher.

I KNOW WHAT LOVE IS

What if the angels,
with their conch-shaped trumpets,
their dainty bows and arrows,
don't really give a shit about us?
What if they gather in heavenly circles
at the mouth of the clouds
to stare down on field mice,
on ferrets, on millipedes?
We think angels take human shape
because our ancestors painted them that way,
but those were the same ancestors
who toiled through the Dark Ages,
who took a long damn time to discern
that the heart wasn't the seat of intelligence.
I'd say they suffered at times
from a lack of imagination.
Sure, they fashioned rocks into the tips of spears,
sure, they managed some empires,
and sure, they figured out
which knotweeds would dye the wool,
which berries would pigment the oils.
Make, if you want, a case for human ingenuity,
but I vote against us
when it comes to knowledge of the Divine.
In Chronicles, God sends an angel
to slaughter the Assyrian army.
In Numbers, he opens chasms
to swallow the defiant,
he burns with holy fire those gathered in worship,
he sets a plague on fourteen thousand.
Imagine writing those words, thinking,
Yes, this is the God who loves me.
I don't think He much cares about us.

I think the next tornado, the next tsunami,
the next antibiotic-resistant strain
will be whimsy and afterthought.
I think He's the God of Rats,
the God of Ticks, surrounded
in heaven by legions of slim-thoraxed angels
flapping swallowtail wings, spitting venom
into each other's many-prismed eyes.
I think He's created the virus in his own image,
and He loves the virus enough
to create an endlessly adaptable food source for it
that also serves as means of conveyance.

BAD NEWS FOR MORTALS IN FORESTS

If I could be a god, I too would descend
in the form of an eagle, a swan. I too
would adopt plumage, lustrous black
and brilliant, stained in early evening
a deep purple, the color of ink under vinegar.
I too would be sour. I too would glide
over boulders and dunes on violet breezes,
interrogating the wind for its secrets.
I too would trick my wife into transforming
into a fly and swallow her, even if she fashioned
in my head not just a suit of armor
but a toy army of mechanical men,
the racket and clanging of a thousand anvils
smithing the space between my ears.
I too would agree to have my head split
upon an axe, if only to see what would spring
forth fully formed – though, in my case,
no daughter would, just a thousand tin clocks,
orderly and automated, ticking away seconds
with clenched fists and puckered faces.
And on the hours, they would spout
tiny copper eagles, bronze swans.
I too would return to Olympus, laurel
and throne, to await the inevitable moment
when I would grow bored with those children,
because I too would grow bored.
Twilight would send its whispers, its itches,
and I would once again take wing.

BELIEVER, AFFIX A FISH TO YOUR SUV

Jesus is love but never more so
than on the highway, when he delivers us
from mid-size sedans unto our destinations.

When he absolves us of our emissions.
I want an anti-lock, all-weather Christ
to emerge after three days in the median.

Believer, evangelism requires a little asphalt,
a little balm for the road rage of the travelers
who passed their injured neighbor before

the Good Samaritan gave roadside assistance.
I need a Ford-tough Savior to perform
certain miracles: pay the tolls in their wicked plazas,

abolish the speed traps in the temple,
truck courageous into eternal sunrise.
I want Hot Rod Yahweh, Jr. to rev the engine

of my love for fellow motorists,
a love I forget a little more with each on-ramp,
every parking lot, any time someone

putters along at 53 on an Interstate.
May he bless me, Turnpike Christ, as he raises
his hands to embrace the long handles of the chopper.

May he anoint me in motor oil, forgive me
for buying Japanese. May he learn to love
me again after I've taken his name in vain

or wished a wreck upon the tailgater,
may he make faith easy as a decal
and carry me past the overpasses,

one set of tread marks screeching safely to halt
when there should have been two.

HEAVENLY BODIES

Someone has torn open a stuffed animal
and released the white entrails
into a strong headwind.
Poor bunny, poor bear,
let this be consolation:
what was inside you grew large
and is streaming across the sky
in the hurricane's aftermath.

The skies shifting, tumbling,
I realize what astronomers knew
centuries ago, before they were burned
at the stake for heresy:
the skies are fixed bodies,
the world is turning. It's just faster
this morning. Here is my dilemma:
the world is spinning quickly north to south.
I am in my car doing sixty, east to west.

I cannot arrive at my destination,
and if I did, could I conclude the business
I'd find there?

This must be how the Beatles felt
in their adventures through Pepperland:
reduced to their cartoon selves,
following the insides of animals
forming the shapes of animals
in the skies.

I cannot stop dreaming and driving.
Wake me from my bucket seat.

I am in danger of crashing,
of finding out the metal will disassemble,
the doors fly off, the windshield ascend,
of finding out I was never driving at all,
of finding out I was never really here.
I am in danger of being a cloud,
the insides, still inside, of an animal
being dragged through mud by a child.

A ROMAN

And hung there, uncooked meat in his teeth,
muttering *Hosannah. Hallelujah. Mea culpa*.

And pressed back the welts in his palms,
ragtag red lions raised on his skin.

But lamented his suffering aloud to the Lord,
who hears the human body as instrument.

The dried blood, tangle in the thatch of beard,
matted sap above cuts in the chest's lush garden.

The trembling at mouth's edge, the weak-knees,
the weak-lung, neck-droop, the voice and knell.

Would not have sung louder wearing thorns.
Would not have sung louder in limp robes.

How colossal the error. How dire. How divine
a breath, a breath, a breath, a breath.

NOTES ON THE ORACLE

Who was the Oracle before the tremors,
before the rupture of the future into her mind's eye?
Was she still a child when she began seeing
the drowning man, the hanging man,
the man split through the sternum by lance,
the burning bodies at the mouth of a cave?
And if so, how does a child
return after such seeing
to the world of childish things,
to dolls made of sticks and a bit of hay?

Divination by chicken gizzards.
Divination by the throat of a lamb.
Divination by a stone in water.
By a wand swung low, by a willow rod,
by a forked tongue, by an eye on sunset,
by blood from a goat, by coin in a fountain,
by buried strands of hair.

If we did not want so badly to believe
we have a future, we would not bring
the sacrifice required
for someone else to see it.

Prophets on hilltops, cloistered in huts,
scrying in sands on smooth marble tabletops.

Gods in their best human disguises,
running through wildernesses with fawns.

The merchant woman in the village
who reads tarot cards,
but deals only the hanged man,
who gazes at the crystal, but sees only haze.

Bring coin to any.
Any will tell you what you want to hear.
And still the news is never good.

≈

Divination by onomancy, by oneiromancy,
divination by runecasting, burning writing onto bark,
tracing the ridges in breastbone,
augury, kaballah, patterns in wax, lots.

≈

The voice of the future, however imperfectly worded,
cleaves the listener with the baritone of authority.
How possibility is a fugue
but certainty is a melody which the listener,
having heard just a bar or two,
endlessly repeats atop the cacophony.

≈

Beware the sacrifices beneath her temple,
not for any menace they may still offer –
none remains – but for the lesson:
when the oracle trades flesh

for a vision, she doesn't specify an offering.
Any carcass will satisfy the seeker
convinced he needs to know
what he will hear. A goat. A dove.
Any traveler in the party.

Divination by ash from incense,
divination by bamboo, divination by basins of water,
by the flight paths of birds, by numbers, by navels,
by pebbles, by the moles on a neck,
by the hook of a scapula.
Divination by accidents. By the placement
of the wounded in an accident.
By the severity of the wounds.
By the cause and site of the accident.
By the time the wounded take to heal,
by the number of wounded who do not,
by the way people whisper of the accident.

And if the child Oracle does return to the doll,
how long will she love it for its human qualities?

SCORPION

This is my fable,
so at the end, I must reply

It is my nature.
You know this story.

The wide river,
the forceful current

rushing like brush fire
across a parched plain.

Your calm strokes
toward the other shore.

I always loved you
for your tenderness,

for your faith in me.
I asked you so many times

carry me on your back.
I wanted to be a crab.

I wanted to be more
like you, less like myself.

Ask me for mercy
at the end of this fable,

ask me for mercy
so I may sting you again.

VS. WORLD

If I were careening down Broadway dressed in my Sunday suit.
If my arms were out to either side, my hands extended.
If my eyes shut, my head tilted.
If my coruscating smile, the kind you'd see in an advertisement.
If roses sloughed off my back and outstretched arms.
If streamers and ribbons followed, and the air aglitter.
If the light fell such that no one in New York cast a shadow.
If I were followed by wolves and playful malamutes,
if the wolves wore velvet collars and the malamutes red kerchiefs.
If I spun.
If confetti in a million different colors from the skyscrapers.
If every window in Manhattan open, and the crowds roaring.
If the people on the curbs and streetcorners tried to reach out to me,
if they clapped, if they pointed, if they whistled.
If everyone on the streetcorners wore fedoras and bowlers,
if everyone had elbow patches on their coats.
If I were in slow-motion, ecstatic and followed by wolves.
If the roses and rosepetals littered the streets behind me.
If all of Manhattan, made of rosepetal.
If I had no one to share it with.
If I had no one I had to share it with.

EXPERT ADVICE FOR YOUR BOXING CAREER

In a parallel space, you and I are boxing,
ring spattered with last night's blood, the
wreck of our loved ones. In a gym miles
wide, clusters of rings: showcases for the
pugilism that infects us, the maniac gene,
our heads tilted downward, your hazel
eyes fixed on forward plane. Why the
sport of hurt remains: what is beautiful
must be beaten beautiful.

IF I DON'T BLACK OUT

The secret is to swallow cities whole,
drink from the gulch after floodwaters come,
make a nest of stars to safely pass night
and emerge fresh in the morning. Drink beer

by the barrel, gin by the distillery,
smoke fields of tobacco wrapped in muslin.
Live like a titan until living
kills you. Cronus sent mammoth

clouds streaming across continents
with a single breath. Theia birthed
the moon. Why be terrified
of the afterlife? It could be high school

in Kansas, bunker floors in need of mopping,
cubicles full of actuaries, miles of ramen.
Not hell, but neither harps and tin halos.
Not a new haircut, per se. Just a trim.

OCEAN QUAHOG

Researchers in Wales say they have discovered the world's oldest living creature –
a 405-year-old clam
  – ABC News

Done counting rings, scientists claim the clam
has lived four centuries. Poor sod, all that time,
he never planned a trip, just mouth open
to where the currents took him.
That's a long time to lug a home around,
but home is where the heart, kidney, and anus are,
wherever the open circulatory system pumps.
He deserves credit for persistence, but acknowledge
the difficulty of a clam giving up. How would it look
any different? Left in his bed, in the arctic deep,
long enough, undisturbed by shark or squid,
living must be the surrender.

IN 27D

After hours of delay
and a particularly long layover,

the voice promising me clear blue skies
sounds like I imagined God

would when he asked me to forgive.
And the stewardess

pushing a cart toward me,
with her smart, ruby lips,

thick eyelashes,
and unconventional snakeskin boots,

looks like I imagined Venus would
if she wagged a finger at me,

inviting me to something forbidden.
Michelangelo's *David*,

on the cover of the in-flight magazine,
flexes the chest I thought I'd have

if I could work shame's nine tails
across my back

enough to diet on grapes
or bike to the gym.

The housefly, the only one
I've ever seen on a plane,

caroming between seatbacks
like a fire drunk on its own heat,

looks like I imagined I might
if I died in a plane crash

and was immediately shuttled back
into the living body I deserve.

If I close my eyes and let the engine noise
drown out all this useless sense,

I can hear Venus as a heron
and see God as a never-ending chest

of drawers, each
one of the infinite shades of blue,

can feel the surprising litheness
of stretched snakeskin,

and smell brush burning
on the prairie,

and my next body is the wavering sunlight
through the surface of water.

THE DAM AT PARCO NAZIONALE DEL GRAN PARADISO

On a particularly precarious section of the dam
seven alpine ibexes balance –
four hooves stacked on a single stone –
scaling the crags that jut from cement,
hundreds of feet above a manmade valley,
licking for salt and minerals.

Most of the year, male ibexes prefer lowlands,
the security of the even and level.
The females tend towards higher terrains.
In winter, gripped by a peculiar ecstasy
that glides in on cold winds,
the males scale hill and mountain.

But sometimes, the trip up gets mixed up –
they climb levees instead of cliff-faces,
they discover great basins of placid water
where they should have found promontories
fat with gorgeous lady ibexes in heat.

Maybe when they arrive,
the male ibexes feel as peaceful
as the water in the deep reservoir
they're forced to edge along,
but I can't help feeling disappointment on their behalf.

All that time out on a ledge.

All those times I scaled the wrong dangerous wall
to places with names like *Great Paradise*,
sniffing at some promise,
some companionship.

How like a goat I felt
on the treacherous trip back down
to whatever hole I was living in.

TRESPASSES

I beg, saints,
call my name.
These are the rules

of engagement.
My worshipful mouth,
wet with

anticipation.
The long aisle,
obscured by doves.

Sunlight streams in,
polychromatic,
and hot.

I buried myself
in red robes,
expectant

at velvet altar.
A cross.
A basin.

Forgive me, saints,
call my name out,
make it echo

the chamber,
the antechamber.
Forgive me Lord,

my wet mouth heaves.
I ask it
without Your

permission.
These are the rules
of attraction.

STATUES OF WOMEN

Presumably to let go of grief,
a man is carving in his back yard a statue of a woman.

His statue is identical to another statue of a woman,
which he saw once in an Italian museum

on a day when sunlight spilled through the stained glass
of a cathedral less than a mile away.

The sunlight fell through the cathedral windows
in magnificent colors, making the dust appear to dance.

The dust, kicked up by the vicar, seemed
to a woman in the front pew to dance.

The cathedral air, which had before seemed stale,
suddenly buoyed her.

Held captive a few moments by the majesty
of dust, in so many colors, dancing,

the dance she supposed another symbol
to indicate the love of her Creator,

the woman in the front pew took the same pose
as the statue of a woman in the Italian museum,

the statue of a woman the man now reproduces
on an awkward patch of his garden.

The woman from the front pew, though she has never met
the man now carving in his back yard a statue,

might have been, for him, the one perfect love
we all suppose we are destined for.

The man passed the woman from the front pew
last year, in an airport in Cologne.

Their eyes met, and lingered, briefly,
and though the man passed her last year,

it is not the likeness of the woman from the front pew,
nor is it the likeness of the woman captured

in the statue he once saw in an Italian museum,
that stirs in him the urge to chip and shape.

He cannot, if asked, tell you quite why
he chisels out of the slab

the same image of a woman another man once chiseled,
or why, when the original was clearly born

of such love, his should be carved of sorrow.

PAST PERFECT

Each time the ferryman
                              reaches the green shores,
his hand so stiff he must pry it from the oar,

he no longer knows himself.
His ashen skin, ashen eyes,
the lingering scent

                    of loss that perfumes him:
he cannot explain them.

Nor do the townspeople recognize him.

He knows only that he arrived
in a modest vessel

                        whose weathered teak
laps up the salt, whose bleached frames

arch over the outside of the hull
as though molding the ship into place,
                          and pull at the weak surf.

Each time,
            he invents a new past,
a story that could be true, if only

because he believes in limits
to what a man can fabricate.

In one, he is a king's sentry in exile,
in another, a good-hearted merchant seeking a young bride –

each tale has some form of complication,
a hitch which explains
                              the tired downward curl
at the edge of his mouth,

                    his battered
and calloused hands.

                    Whatever the tale
he settles on, he settles into it, he believes it.
He finds lodging. He suppers.

The townspeople believe it too,
his counterfeit of a life lived,
until one,
                    overcome with grief, walks the shore

and recognizes the ivory contours of his boat.

Word spreads through town
on hoarse voices.
                    Soon all the mourning know.
Soon

        the boldest of the bereaved approaches him,
perhaps at a tavern, where he downs an ale,

perhaps already on the docks,
securing a rigging for a voyage
                              he's begun to sense he must take.

When the bereaved places a coin
in his rough palm,

                    the invented past dissipates,
as if it were a vapor, a fog seared away:
he sees clearly his ship's frames

as the ribs of a skeleton.

Silently, then, he loads his freight,
                                    turns the boat
back toward that same obscene shore,

drags the oar across the water
                            in the shapes of letters,
hoping to write the book of his dread,

one he can read as he paddles in return.

THE SKUNK

In the grieving house,
the hot water tap runs cold.
The mice quiet.
Shoes in neat pairs in the top dresser drawer.
No one comes home for dinner.
Incandescents burn in the sitting room,
fluorescents switched off by the porch.

Dying appears sometimes as a man
on skis, a racing inevitability,
and sometimes as the spider Anansi.
But now, it is the skunk.

In the grieving house,
the air tamps down.
The kitchen smells like cedar.
The foyer smells like cedar.
The bedroom smells like cedar.

EXPERT ADVICE FOR YOUR DAY AT THE TRACK

There's time in this life for horse-racing,
but so little. Time is always fully automatic,
measured not in units but in the space
between finishes. You can tell a horse
anything to make him race – a fable, a white
lie, a deep-held democratic principle –
but he's listening for the whip-snap of
raised air before the crop strikes. He can
tell you anything, too, and it won't make
you head home. The parking lot is full of
Lincolns, brown cars, sad lampposts. You
don't want to go there. Stake another. Love
was a horse in the seventh, passed through
the gates limp. No one talks about the
horse pulled up lame when we're settling
down to dinner, saddled, jockeys on our
backs. We're rode hard, and too slow across
the finish line. All save one.

WONDERS NEVER CEASE

All day bees built honeycombs
around the sleepers,

    weaving wax
into hexagons, laying in honey,
sealing the walls.

  Work which might
have taken months,
       all in an afternoon.

The sleepers dreamed of corn cobs
and race cars,
    of Egyptian burial rituals.

The dreams were fitful, but the sleepers
hardly shifted
   as thin wings sputtered
around them, larvae maturing in minutes.

The sleepers slept peacefully,
their arms crossed
  as though
they had been laid,
  lifeless,
in a pharaoh's tomb.

Each of us has only minutes left to live.

Ruin lies in rushing through.

GHAZAL

I need to feel the lash as you beat me out of me,
the white knuckle across my cheekbone as you beat me out of me.

If I seem like I want to be insensible, I am ready to leave
this body, ready to ascend to star if you beat me out of me.

Ready for a lung collapse. I will accept any form of brutality
as payment. I will beg you to beat me. Out of me,

nothing good will grow. No dogwood. No forsythia.
I am salt in soil, poison ground. Beat me out of me

so that I may forget I ever was. Concuss me,
retrograde amnesia me. Beat me out of me.

When I was a boy, my father said that the last one to woods' edge
would drive the devil's automobile. He beat me out. Of me,

of my preoccupation with the devil, he could barely speak.
He locked me in a distant cabin. Please, beat me out of me

and my tendency to remember. Reality is so fucking fickle
sometimes. It will be the cudgel that beats me out of me,

then hammers me back in. Loose nail. Faulty wiring.
Nothing is right. It is why I ask you to beat me out of me,

that I may be anyone but my self-obsessed self,
preening like a white seal. Beat me out of me

with the violence you have only just discovered
you needed. The devil steers. I am him. Beat me out of me.

THOUGH WE THREATEN TO LOWER THE HAMMER, WE COME TO LOVE IT IN TIME

A toad took up residence on a wood slat
        by the back door. We nudged him

with our feet; he did not stir.
        We lit matches and held them close;

he did not leap. We leaned down
        to look him in the eye, we shouted;

he did not startle. Stillness
        was his camouflage. He must have believed

everything he'd heard about people.
        His black eyes like obsidian under water

reflected back our worst impulses.
        You raised your foot above him and said,

I am a hammer. I am the hammer of God.
        But you did not bring it down.

Eventually we brought him a leaf of lettuce,
        an old cottage cheese container

full of water. You wanted to sugar the water.
        I said no. Later that night there was lightning,

the crooked kind of lightning
        that tells a story of an empty savannah.

He was gone in the morning.
        He was so familiar, you said.

Then why did you want to harm him, I asked.
You did not reply. Later, you painted

a thresher behind a goatherd and goat.
We recognize in each other

a certain stubbornness.

SECOND LOVE

I took you nowhere,
still shellshocked from the carpet bombing

      at the end of first love,
still in awe of how quick
the turn from roses to reproach,

      the hollowing out.

For third love, I laid shingles on rooftops,
I moved across country in a semi-stolen camper,
      I skinnydipped in quarries
in each of the Western states;

for fourth love, I married.

But all you got was codependence,
      occasional chrysanthemums.

I promise I was trying
but the itinerary was blank –

first love, I took to magnificent bridges
      where we dangled our feet
and talked about how far the drop would be,

third love, I steered toward the stone cities,
the curious mausoleums
we could not wait to explore,
full of bones, tarnished silver,

fourth love, I flew to villas in green mountains,
        to Parisian avenues,
vast museums.

Second love, I delivered you
        to the desert –
                I had to be sure
I wouldn't remember any of the landmarks.

MISDIRECTION

We lay on a ratty blanket
by the pond in the back yard.
You faced the water to watch
ripples set off by the skimmers.
I faced out toward the trees,
waiting for clarity after months of grief.
You whispered, *Nothing about reality*
seems fuzzy anymore.
We were still for a time.
Two clouds crept away from each other,
and the moon laid thin white enamel
over your skin, pinpricks in your eyes.
I could see the shapes of herons
against the lightening sky.
Behind you, three albino deer
took tentative steps toward us.
They lurched when you sighed
and said, *It's the world.*
All the magic has gone out of it.
You never saw them.
I found I could not respond.
I had doves, like refugees
from a handkerchief
or false-bottomed hat,
in my throat.

LAST SONNET FOR MY BELOVEDS

At the end of the relationship,
we were not sour.

I was the apple, you were the plum.
Or you were the cowbird, I was the nest.

We could not be apart together.

Sweet invader, I was the wrong country,
I was the stronghold, I was the armory.
Or you were the charity, you were the bed,
you were the bill folded into a palm,
and I was the indigent too proud.

Still I see you in every passing taxi.
Still I see you engraved
on the world, wearing a bracelet
given to you by another lonely month.

A MOVIE IN WHICH SOMEONE FALLS TO HIS DEATH

Concerning the body
that has taken up residence
on my sofa, that is me.

I hardly recognize myself
there, either, with those arms
and those legs, those ugly sprouts.

The doctors told me I had a concussion
but my head is the only piece
of me not woozy.

I needed to watch a movie
in which someone does not fall to his death.
I could not find one.

A body could learn a lot
from observing the bodies of monkeys
unwound and breathing.

Therefore, I have taken
to practicing a form of yoga
based on primate behavior.

I have taken to penitence
for all my other actions
based on primate behavior.

I continue to wonder
where my stuntman is
and how he will put out this fire.

I continue to hold out hope
that when my stuntman arrives,
I will discover he is me.

DAMNED IF YOU DO AND DAMNED IF YOU DO

Today was harder. I was barely a creature,
my fangs filed down, my claws jagged and caught in the carpet.
        I took a lot of comfort
in the misfortune of others.
My favorite colleague resigned
so I claimed his office chair, its lumbar supports
and adjusting swivel –
Oh Lord, it feels good to just be comfortable
with this tail, these scales, these feathers.
Clothes never fit them right.
I can never find enough meat to satisfy,
never enough heat to keep January from my bones.
        I will be asked to recant
my statement as soon as I'm in the company of others,
the ones holding batons, wearing jackboots,
the blue costumes of the bored.
The stories of salvation are boring –
        it's all a lot of bread
and dirt and daguerreotypes,
a sort of heaven for great-grandparents.
We're taught early on to want what we do not want,
to treasure what we can always have.
Vegetables before we leave the table,
        fluoride in the water.
I was in the future most of yesterday
but now I am in the past tomorrow.
The director tells me to figure it out,
to find the emotion, but I've found so much of it
that I've chosen to cease feeling entirely.
        I'm chewing the scenery,
clawing the black sheet over the window to shreds.

NOW DEPARTING

If, suitcase thrown open on the bed,
I stare, dead-eyed like Pacific salmon,
uncertain where to begin packing,
do not stop chattering. Do not become sullen.

I do not travel lightly. I am the torn-toed sock
everywhere but home: nagging
and uncomfortable, only one purpose
and failing at that. Toss a rock
in the suitcase. Throw a harpoon
into the dumb O of my gaping mouth.

Or, like a siren, sing me to sleep,
fold me over my own limp body,
and pack me away. Mothball me good.

Ship me to the prescribed destination
without any of my comforts, shock my system
when unpacking me into a foreign apartment,
so thoroughly that the only familiar, you,
will be enough to forget the washcloths,
the nail clippers in the bedside table,
the third pair of slippers, fourteenth of shoes.

The plane tickets are on the dresser.
Take pains to set the lights on a timer.

A SHOEBOX

You can lollygag all you want around the small flame but you
better pay attention to the five-alarm fire.
— my father

But the small flames,
   bobbing at the tip
   of the wick to stay alight,
   swaying like charmed snakes
   aware they will soon be caught —
those are the ones I cannot take my eyes from.
I'm fascinated by the little dangers,
   & how easily they can be extinguished:
      a thumb & forefinger pressed against the wick,
      a sudden rush of air.

When I see a blue jay with a clipped wing,
   or a cardinal with a broken foot,
you can sound the sirens, let loose a mighty yowl,
   or bang the pots & pans on an aluminum garbage can,
   but I only hear that wounded chirp.

I trace my finger, if my patient will let me,
   over the curve of the beak,
I nurse it from a dropper,
& I coo to it as it sleeps on a blanket
   I've prepared in a shoebox.
I sing the nightingale song of the damaged,
   the torch anthem of the weak.
It is a simpler song, fewer alarms than five:
   a couple of notes, a trill vocal.

I can hardly see sky without envisioning
   how the invalids in my care will fill it,

flutter & wing, cautious at first,
then jubilant in flight
after weeks nestled in comfort.
But when they have healed,
I hesitate to throw open the doors,
to shake the makeshift manger
& loose them among the crows,
the sparrows, all those little dangers.

& sometimes, when I am close to sleep,
when I am almost to the city
where my convalescents gather
to fly garlands around my head,
my wife will lay the back of her hand lightly
across my temple, she will look down
at me in the flickering light
from the candle she keeps at the bedside,

& I know that our marriage bed
is the shoebox she set up for me,
& she will wait nights to see if I worsen,
if I fall prey to the small perils,
just enough that she can keep me
from returning to the wild.

YOU ARE FOREVER A VISITOR IN YOUR OWN HOME

Every fortune cookie I crack open
yields a little house for us to live in:
riches, travel, strangers with important messages.
We don't get the same thrill from books,
all promise on the dust jacket but never over
fast enough. We stopped reading before
the honeymoon on Menorca. A man there,
in the sandal store, has never forgotten your smile.
I wonder if he thinks he was promised you.
A psychic told me I would die at fifty-two
of heart trouble. All these other troubles
aren't fatal. I've lived so many places
without ever leaving the house
because all the undiscovered countries
are baked, plastic-wrapped, shipped
across the country we know, boxed,
and delivered with our beef and broccoli.
I'm prone to reckless fits of believing
in you. This last one has lasted years.
We still have boxes in the guest room full
of books we read when we were single;
we no longer need them, we'll never read them
the same, we might enjoy them more now
but aren't willing to find out.
You still have an ex-boyfriend in China
who never shipped your clothes –
you wouldn't wear them in the States, anyhow,
but you'd like the opportunity to show me
before they go to Goodwill. Absence
is the only malice some people have left
to give. But I will be gone in nineteen years

and you can blame the psychic for that
if you don't blame me for believing it.
I promise I meant no harm.
I hope you'll travel to Menorca
to see if anyone else got the fortune I got today:
Soon, a visitor will delight you.
Oh, how you delight me.

AS A DEER APPROACHING A CLEARING
IN THE MEADOW –

as a retiring ballerina,
for whom the arch of the back,
the outstretched toe,
has been a form of speech –

as a Bradford Pear
under the grey expanse
of winter sky,
its knotted limbs
plucked by sleet
of its last stale leaves –

as the lake under moon
after the final ripple
has crawled to water's edge
and submerged –

I find myself
at a quiet nexus:

I am ready to say less.

LEAVING

The New England towns roll by, dotting the valleys,
white churches with stern, Puritan steeples,
a few old farmhouses, parsonages punctuated with belfries.
The turning leaves shout every imaginable orange,
some panicked yellows, while evergreens stand sentry.

This must be what leaving feels like: a passage gouged
into granite mountains, rocks scored with rain.
So often I never left, just abandoned the effort. Today, the bus
is full of somber riders who said goodbyes at the station.
One woman in a wool cap pressed her hand to the window

while the man she was leaving puffed up his chest.
As the coach slowly pulled away, he pantomimed a run
alongside. As the coach gained speed, his exaggerated trot
stretched to full gallop. He tried as long as he could
to keep pace, waving goodbye, until finally she pulled

away the hand, as if to release him of the obligation,
and she craned her head to watch him hunch, panting,
one hand propped on his knees to prop and comfort
the body that could not keep up, the other still waving.
Then she faced forward, and I thought that was maybe

the saddest thing I'd seen in some time, or I was sad
because I was still turned and could see him lowering his hand,
and when he straightened, crossed the street to his car,
he was already living another life. In the median, sprigs
of maple sprout auburn leaves, last buds before winter.

We pass mile markers, signs for places named
for the tribes that once farmed the cold land,

for colonists who displaced them. A creek runs south
alongside the highway for a few miles, wind-blown leaves
the color of fire twirl in the eddies behind slick rocks.

Smoke rises from a few chimneys in the valleys.
One day soon someone else will wonder who built
these towns, who tended the stoves, re-shingled the roofs,
and whether when they left, they left in dead of winter
or while the leaves' red orange said, *Please. It's not over.*

THE OLD GODS

After rain, fog rises from the mountain
like an apparition, the green tips of trees
frosted in nostalgia and heat. Wherever
I see *ghosts*, I think *shame*. All that unfinished
regret.

❧

When I drive through the downpour
I focus so closely on the road I barely see
steeples, the soft curves of courthouse rotundas
peeking through the wilderness below.
Like scars, they're easy after a while not to notice.

❧

I don't believe in reincarnation as described
in gilded murals and worn leathers,
but neither do I believe in ghosts,
only that the past taunts us through its colors
and architectures, the browns and grays
of dust and ash, the rusted girders of yesterdays.

❧

Look at the marvelous statehouse cupola
erected in a valley and consider all its builder
buried beneath. Consider the flood plain
drowned when the new dam was built.
Consider the graves – unmarked, so unmoved.
And what does that consideration get you?

⋙

I'm trying to look ahead only as far
as the torrents will allow instead of staring
into the obscured distances ahead.
I'm trying not to turn around

⋙

                                       as lightning
rips the soft silver flesh of the clouds:
I don't believe we are saved by facing
our truths – though they are seldom
behind us. All that is back there
is the past, drafting its legislation, authoring
its bibles, pouring its foundations
over bone and primitive tool.

⋙

Still, nostalgia is sweet in the ear as it calls,
begging us to coat the steeples in gold,
to bathe the leaves in rosewater and lavender,

⋙

but I have never wanted sweetness. Why else
ride into storm?

⋙

Nor have I ever wanted
the future. I watch the blinking hazard
lights in swirling mist ahead, trying
not to court the moment I've dreamt of
when my heat, too, will linger
like a cloak above the mountain.

᷍

The past calls to us *love, love* and
the future calls to us *come, come*.
The only moment unable to speak
is now: rain between twin yellow lines,
oil pooling on asphalt, the hazards
compiling and potential. Steady
hands on the wheel. Fog in the distance.

ACKNOWLEDGEMENTS

The author would like to gratefully acknowledge the editors of the following magazines in which these poems first appeared, sometimes in earlier versions:

American Literary Review: 'As a Deer Approaching a Clearing in the Meadow – '

American Poetry Review: 'Ghazal', 'Leaving', 'I Know What Love Is', 'Scorpion', 'Statues of Women', 'Trespasses'

Bennington Review: 'The Old Gods'

B O D Y Literature: 'Last Sonnet for My Beloveds', 'Though We Threaten to Lower the Hammer, We Come to Love It in Time'

Carolina Quarterly: 'Now Departing'

The Collagist: 'If I Don't Black Out', 'You Are Forever a Visitor in Your Own Home'

The Cortland Review: 'The Dam at Parco Nazionale del Gran Paradiso'

Day One: 'Misdirection'

Lightning Key Review: 'A Movie in Which Someone Falls to His Death'

Los Angeles Review: 'Second Love'

Nashville Review: 'Believer, Affix a Fish to Your SUV'

New England Review: 'I Like Too Many Things', 'Notes on the Oracle', 'Quae Nocent Saepe Docent', 'The Skunk', 'Two Swans', 'Vs. World'

Nimrod: 'A Shoebox'

Oklahoma Review: 'A Roman'

PANK: 'Expert Advice for Your Boxing Career'

Sixth Annual Nazim Hikmet Poetry Festival Anthology: 'Past Perfect', 'Wonders Never Cease'

The Southern Review: 'Dead Finch', 'In 27D'

storySouth: 'Michelangelo's *David*'

Tinderbox Poetry Journal: 'Damned If You Do and Damned If You Do'

Vinyl Poetry: 'Junk Drawer'

'Heavenly Bodies' was featured with a print by Andy Farkas in an exhibit entitled *The Illustrated Word* at Flanders Art Gallery in 2008. 'Quae Nocent Saepe Docent' and 'Two Swans' were reprinted by *Poetry Daily* (poems.com). 'Michelangelo's *David*' was awarded honorable mention in the 2013 Randall Jarrell Poetry Competition, sponsored by the North Carolina Writers' Network. 'Ocean Quahog' appeared in *Best New Poets 2012*, edited by Matthew Dickman. 'Quae Nocent Saepe Docent' appeared on *One Pause Poetry*. 'Heavenly Bodies' appeared in *The Southern Poetry Anthology, Volume*

VII: North Carolina, edited by William Wright, Paul Ruffin, and Jesse Graves. 'Past Perfect,' 'Quae Nocent Saepe Docent,' 'Scorpion,' and 'Wonders Never Cease' appeared in *Poems from the Heron Clan V*, edited by Doug Stuber and Jonathan York. 'A Roman,' 'Quae Nocent Saepe Docent' and 'The Skunk' appeared in the chapbook *How We Came Upon the Colony* (Unicorn Press, 2014). 'Scorpion,' 'Vs. World,' and 'You Are Forever a Visitor in Your Own Home' appeared in the chapbook *The Polite Society* (Unicorn Press, 2017). 'The Skunk' owes a debt to Jack Kirby. 'Vs. World' owes a debt to Kathryn Hawthorne.

I want to extend tremendous thanks to everyone who helped this collection into the world: Debra Allbery, Kate Arden, Jim Barber, Black Spring Press Group, Emma Bolden, Ellen C. Bush, Gabrielle Calvocoressi, Zena Cardman, Noreen Cargill, Maria Carlos, Brittany Cavallaro, Michael Collier, Kelly Copolo, Jennine Capó Crucet, Julia Kolchinsky Dasbach, Maudelle Driskell, Mary Floyd-Wilson, Vievee Francis, Friends of Writers, Marianne Gingher, The Grind Daily Writing Series, Jennifer Grotz, Yona Harvey, Rebecca Hazelton, Rodney Jones, A. Van Jordan, Sally Keith, Terry L. Kennedy, Mary Leader, the Lindanians, Jamaal May, Nathan McClain, Victoria Lynne McCoy, Michael McFee, Heather McHugh, Wade Minter, Elizabeth Moose, Ashley Nissler, Andi & John Pearson, Carl Phillips, Matthew Poindexter, Kevin Prufer, Martha Rhodes, David Rivard, Andrew Saulters, Mike Scalise, Elizabeth Scanlon, Alan Shapiro, Bland Simpson, Mary Snyders, Beverly Spicer, Noah Stetzer, the students who have taught me so much, Arthur Sze, Melissa Thibault, Peter Turchi, Reed Turchi, Ellen Bryant Voigt, Daniel Wallace, Bill White, C. Dale Young, Katie Bowler

Young, and everyone – a legion of peers, editors, and friends – who generously offered feedback on these poems and boundless encouragement. This collection would not have been possible without the support of the MFA Program at Warren Wilson College, the Bread Loaf Writers' Conference, the staff and trustees at The Frost Place, the Durham Arts Council, the North Carolina Writers' Network, the University of North Carolina at Chapel Hill, and the North Carolina School of Science and Mathematics.

My eternal gratitude to Lloyd Schwartz for choosing this collection for the Sexton Prize.

Dilruba Ahmed and Matthew Olzmann, it never happens without you.
Heidi White, I wouldn't want it to.